NEW ZEALAND

TOWN AND COUNTRY GARDENS

Photographs by Gil Hanly
Text by Julian Matthews

David Bateman

Published in 1993 by
David Bateman Ltd, "Golden Heights",
32-34 View Road, Glenfield,
Auckland, New Zealand

ISBN 1 86953 155 8

Designed by Errol McLeary
Typeset by Typeset Graphics, Auckland
Printed in Hong Kong by Colorcraft Ltd

Contents

Introduction

L ast spring, as I travelled the country on my annual pilgrimage gathering material on great gardens and the fascinating folk who create them, I kept meeting up with Gil Hanly. I knew Gil was taking photographs for a book, but it never crossed my mind that she was contemplating asking me to do the text.

The invitation came a few weeks later, when Gil knocked on my door very early one morning. She was on her way home from weeks on the road covering South Island gardens. Over a cup of coffee, I was invited to join the project. My involvement with *New Zealand Gardener* magazine is so time consuming that I would have said no to anyone else, but such is my regard for Gil's ability with a camera that I could only accept; and try not to think of the late nights to come.

All the hard work produced a book which I feel is a tribute to the very high standard of gardening in New Zealand, and to the artistry of Gil Hanly.

Diana and Brian Anthony, 'Valley Homestead and Gardens', Whangarei.

Diana and Brian Anthony have turned gorse into garden in just six years. And what a garden it is, overflowing with bright flowers set off to perfection by the sombre green of surrounding native forest. Diana, labelled Mighty Mouse by Brian because of Herculean efforts with spade and crowbar, has planted lots of old roses and perennials which suit the century-old kauri homestead to perfection. Free-flying white pigeons add to the fairytale feel of this very special place.

Opposite: The breathtaking combination of 'Albéric Barbier' framing the window, meeting up with the cupped pink flowers of 'Raubritter' says it all about the romance and beauty of old roses. The aptly named lobster plant (*Beloperone guttata*), extremely free flowering in the mild Northland climate, grows at the foot of 'Raubritter'.

Below right: An old tree is host to the rose 'Sparrieshoop' and *Clematis montana*. The latter, a glorious sight in mid spring, is showing a few of its last flowers.

Following pages: A corner of the serene pond, home to beautiful waterlilies and lotus. In summer it's a cool spot to escape the heat of the Northland sun, in winter a romantic place where one can linger in the nearby gazebo and watch the first raindrops of a passing storm ruffling the calm surface.

Visitors arriving by car have to concentrate carefully to avoid being distracted by the dazzling colours of the gardens beside the drive which are set off by the deep green of background trees. The old roses 'Sombreuil' and 'Buff Beauty' clamber over the gazebo, combining with brilliant orange watsonias at the side.

Alison and Doug McRae, 'Chindie', Otorohanga.

Alison's country garden started out small and grew along with her enthusiasm. Five times Doug removed the fences further into the paddocks and on each occasion Alison skilfully blended the old with the new by moving in established trees as the framework for her extended plantings. The garden, which features lots of camellias, rhododendrons and natives, is a peaceful place, with water to soothe the soul and native birdsong to further enhance the celebration of nature.

Opposite: One of several ponds in the garden, with the red foliage of *Nandina domestica* 'Pygmaea' making a bright splash of colour.

The brilliant big blooms of *Rhododendron* 'College Pink' are eagerly awaited each spring.

Below: Strategically placed ornaments such as this little statue among the ferns are a hallmark of the garden. The prolific soft-pink rhododendron is 'Party Dress'.

Susan and Richard Macfarlane, 'Winterhome'.

In an age when the soft flowing lines of cottage gardens are the height of fashion, 'Winterhome' is daringly different. This amazing garden, which makes full use of plants suited to the dry Marlborough climate, is big and bold,

Delectable delphiniums beside the house. Variations of the blue, mauve and white theme, so appropriate to the cloudless skies of Marlborough, are replayed throughout the garden.

Right: The formal rose bed accommodates eighty bushes of the very free flowering 'Margaret Merril'. On warm summer evenings the heady scent of this strongly fragrant rose drifts on the air, putting one in mind of romantic twilights on tropical isles.

with a stunning vista stretching away from the house, huge brick walls with espaliered apple trees, and expansive sea views good enough to make a Hollywood film director swoon.

A dramatic vista terminates at the white seat. Clipped box (buxus) provides the straight edges essential to the design, backed up by lavender.

Left: The raised pond in front of the house, with wide sides which encourage one to sit daringly close on hot summer days and play with the soothing water.

Barbara and Robert Walker, Te Kuiti.

Barbara is a passionate gardener who works in a nursery during the week and spends weekends and summer evenings creating gorgeous scenes with her own plants. The grand house was built in 1907 and the magnificent trees which provide a framework for the garden date back to that time. It's not easy rebuilding an old garden, but Barbara has achieved something very special with her re-creation of formal areas in front of the house and new landscaping of the hillside below.

Below: Old trees which have had their day make way for exciting new plantings.

Opposite: Hardy heaths clipped into bun shapes are a fun design feature.

A celebration of spring: scarlet mollis azaleas and the blue forget-me-not-like flowers of *Cynoglossum nervosum*.

Shirley and Peter Lowes, 'Rapaura Watergarden', Tapu.

Just one pond can add a touch of magic to a garden, so you can imagine the enchantment at Rapaura Watergarden where there are fourteen ponds, some of them very large, all in pristine settings. There's a waterfall too, reached by a bush track. The regenerating bush backdrop (the valley in which the garden lies was logged for kauri as late as 1929) adds to the feel that this is a very natural place. It's not surprising to learn that Shirley and Peter employ biodynamic techniques in the garden as part of their quest to be at one with nature.

Opposite: The blue pickerell rush *(Pontederia cordata)* and waterlilies provide colour in the water while on land tree ferns and bamboos create a lush tropical look.

A bit of whimsy on the edge of the bush. The purple flowers of Spanish shawl *(Heterocentron elegans)* contrast with the subtle colours of native ferns.

Below: A wonderful expanse of waterlilies in the largest ponds and a tree-fern-clothed hill as the backdrop.

Faith and Rodney Wilson, 'Cross Hills', Kimbolton.

When the late Eric Wilson retired from farming towards the end of the 1960s he looked for an interesting project to work on and, like many a person at that stage of life, took to gardening with enthusiasm. But Eric didn't confine himself to a small house garden, as might have been expected, choosing instead to turn farm paddocks into one of the world's most notable rhododendron gardens. Today, 'Cross Hills' rhododendron garden is run by Eric's son Rodney and his wife Faith. Every year they open the gates to more than ten thousand visitors who come to celebrate the feast of colour.

A planting of hardy heathers and callunas provides an interesting contrast in form and foliage to a bank of rhododendrons.

Left: Woodland areas at Cross Hills feature tall rhododendrons which dazzle the thousands of springtime visitors.

Opposite: The waterfall is a new and very popular feature. The upper reaches of the bank are clothed with *Clematis montana* varieties 'Rubens' and 'Tetrarose'.

Following pages: The deciduous azalea dell, the most colourful of all the features in this spectacular garden, with the highly scented white *Rhododendron lindleyi* providing a snowy contrast.

Nicki and Clive Higgie, 'Paloma', Fordell.

Lots of palms, bamboos and flamboyant flowers incorporated into a garden which has been designed with panache and originality. It sounds like the sort of thing one would expect in the grounds of an expensive Hawaiian resort hotel, but Clive and Nicki have achieved their tropical paradise in the countryside near Wanganui. The tropical feel of the garden is astonishing, as is the fact that its creation has been fitted in with busy work schedules and raising a family.

Above right: The bold succulent *Agave attenuata* makes a striking wall plant beneath a grove of washingtonia palms.

Below right: Towering flower spikes of *Echium pininiana* and the huge shiny green leaves of native puka *(Meryta sinclairii)* provide a dramatic background for succulents in a sun baked part of the garden.

Opposite: Big bromeliads *(Aechmea cordata)* beneath washingtonia palms are typical of the tropical look characteristic of this astonishing garden.

Lee and Graham Dunster, 'Hui Hui', Hawarden.

'Hui Hui' is a spectacular high-country garden which makes the most of features such as a little lake where black swans and other exciting birds make their homes. It's a new garden, but has the advantage of established trees which were once a feature of the old homestead. Colour schemes are carefully thought out — whites near the house, bold colours around the gazebo, red autumn colouring trees beside the lake for dramatic reflections. Lots of flowering cherries are a feature of spring, their white flowers drifting on the gentle breezes like snowflakes.

Top left: Lots of white flowers have been planted near the house. The rose 'Moonlight', a sweetly scented hybrid musk, features on the brick wall with white cistus and blue catmint at the base.

Left: The deep, still waters of the lake provide a placid backdrop to the garden. Hostas, bearded irises, heucheras and lupins make a pretty waterside group.

Opposite: Lee's interest in colour combinations is evident in this area which she calls her "pucey garden". The inspired group consists of a bright pink rhododendron, coral heuchera, hot pink cistus and inky purple lupins.

Following pages: Lupins were intended as just a quick means of filling up a new area but Lee fell in love with them, despite the fact that her asthma flares up when they bloom, and they have become an impressive feature.

A perfect example of why native
Clematis paniculata is considered one of
the world's top ornamental climbers.
Here it thrives with a cool root run and
a diet of compost galore plus old stable
manure.

Sue and Gerald Spratt, 'Kwaint Acres', Te Puke.

Sue loves climbers and her garden is full of ponga arches built to display them to perfection. Her garden is also notable for its ponds and bog areas, where moisture-loving irises have free rein, and masses of old roses which turn the late spring into a feast for the eyes and nose.

Opposite: A big weeping elm provides a natural sun umbrella much appreciated by guests at summer barbecues.

Below: Shell paths lead among plants chosen for their interesting form as much as their flowers. In the foreground a wiry native coprosma contrasts with Solomon's seal and on the other side deep pink primulas stand out against the blue-grey leaves of *Hosta sieboldiana*.

Ro and John Worley, 'Little Otahome', Masterton.

Ro's strong ideas on design have made 'Little Otahome' one of the most distinctive gardens in the country. The use of tightly clipped hedges and a preoccupation with the form of plants means that hers is a garden of year-round interest, but in spring when the colour co-ordinated flowers are at their peak everything comes together and the result stops you in your tracks, as great designs always do.

Opposite: Long borders are planted with groups of annuals, perennials and roses, skilfully grouped to make a colour co-ordinated picture.

Below: Hedges (in this instance *Lonicera nitida*) are used extensively in the garden, providing strong form and year-round interest.

The gravel path with its lush plantings either side echoes the stream with its grassy banks which runs through the garden.

Pam Wratten, 'Lavender Patch', Lower Moutere.

Pam's garden is really two gardens — an enchanted mixture of trees and perennials close to the pretty house and a wide open space full of hundreds of lavender bushes. English lavender is harvested and made into a range of traditional products which are sold to visitors who come in the spring and summer. Those who come to be enchanted by the lavender are greeted

A sea of lavender and contrasting flower spikes of giant *Echium pininana*.

Left: Big trees close to the house create a fairytale effect much appreciated by children. Pam was delighted when a little boy who came to visit said, "You live in a jungle — boy it's neat."

by a sign which reads, "Feel free to squeeze and smell the lavenders — Pam". Soft coloured old-fashioned roses grow on the edge of the lavender beds, adding to the pot pourri of fragrances.

Right: Favourites among the lavenders are 'Hidcote', which keeps its colour best when dried, and 'Munstead' which is loved for its ethereal look in the garden.

Below: Little courtyards give a very intimate feel to the house garden. The climbers are an ornamental grape and the white-flowered rose 'Félicité et Perpétue'.

Olive Dunn, 'Foresta Fragrant Garden', Invercargill.

Olive ran a highly successful florist's shop in Invercargill for many years. In retirement her considerable energy and artistic abilities have been devoted to developing her garden and sharing it with others through her popular books and articles. Some people say that Olive's garden is like a great big florist's shop, full of fascinating sights and smells, innovative yet always beautiful.

A typical example of Olive's very full, 'cottagey' style of planting, with roses 'Dapple Dawn' (right centre), 'Bantry Bay' and 'Cornelia' (on the gazebo).

Below: The courtyard, with a big tufa pot the crowning glory for a selection of potted plants, most colourful of which are red, pink and white rhodohypoxis. A big honeysuckle provides scent and beauty to the rear and the beautiful white flowers of *Abutilon vitifolium* 'Alba' decorate the foreground.

Opposite: Even in the vegetable garden colour and texture are carefully considered. In the foreground an assortment of lettuces illustrates the point that it's not only ornamentals that are decorative.

'Eastwoodhill Arboretum', Ngatapa, Gisborne.

'Eastwoodhill' is an amazing garden with an even more amazing story. William Douglas Cook devoted much of his life to planting the incredible collection of trees and shrubs, spending a fortune with the world's best nurseries, often gardening naked except for a sunhat and gumboots. He planted until the end of his life, which could also have been the end of this unique property. Fortunately a local farmer, Mr H.B. Williams, purchased the property

As 'Eastwoodhill's' curator, Garry Clapperton, aptly puts it, the arboretum is "an oasis of vegetation in a desert of grassland."

Left: Autumn at 'Eastwoodhill' is an enchanted time of fiery foliage, intense blue skies and soft carpets of rustling leaves underfoot.

45

and subsequently handed it over to The Eastwoodhill Trust Board, thus ensuring the arboretum's future.

Left: The sheltered valleys suit Japanese maples to perfection

Opposite: Douglas Cook used to bury wine beneath trees such as this, sometimes surprising visitors by asking if they would like a drink, then, if they said yes, digging up a bottle and opening it on the spot.

The mixture of evergreen conifers and deciduous trees is a delight at any season, but especially so in autumn.

Left: The reputation of oaks as trees of great beauty is reinforced by this magnificent specimen which makes a dramatic contrast to a hardy palm (Trachycarpus fortunei). There are more than 100 different oaks in the arboretum.

Betty and Charles Moore, 'Westwood', Waitati.

Paths carved through the native bush, rustic bridges spanning sparkling streams, tree ferns providing a canopy for big drifts of primulas, here is an example of a garden with that elusive New Zealand feel to it, little influenced by Northern Hemisphere fashions.

Opposite: Native foliage plants and the bright flowers of rhododendrons make a pleasing combination.

Below: Much of the garden has been created in clearings among native bush.

The Himalayan poppy *(Meconopsis betonicifolia)* thrives in cool, shady corners.

Jacqui and Alastair Sutherland, 'Whangaimoana', South Wairarapa.

Jacqui's garden is like an oasis in an area of low rainfall. In early spring, fields of daffodils bring the crowds flocking from miles around, relishing these symbols of a bright new season. Later in the year the same folk will often return to wander the broad paths edged with lavender, running their hands among the spiky flowers to release the heady perfume as they marvel at towering echiums and drifts of foxgloves. Unlike so many New Zealand gardens this is not a place to see rhododendrons — the plants which grow here have been chosen for their ability to do well in the dry conditions.

Top left: The grey pot with a pretty little daisy bush *(Chrysanthemum mawii)* was planted on the advice of a landscape architect who said if you have an elegant pot put something simple in it. Obviously he knew what he was talking about. The mass of red beyond the stone wall is a pelargonium which used to grow in the garden of Jacqui's mother.

Below left: Californian poppies, love-in-a-mist and the white-flowered shrub *Adenandra uniflora* create a cottage garden effect either side of a path leading to a grand old New Zealand ngaio.

Opposite: Succulents, geraniums, the towering flower spikes of Pride of Madeira *(Echium fastuosum)*, foxgloves, lavender and the 'Perle d'Or' rose provide pathside interest.

Beverley and Malcolm McConnell, 'Ayrlies', Whitford.

It's a tribute to Bev's gardening skills that the lakes, waterfalls and woodlands at 'Ayrlies' look like naturally occurring features. She and Malcolm started in 1964 with an exposed, undulating paddock. The ups and downs of the land provided the opportunity for drama, with vistas from the high spots and intimate areas in the sheltered hollows, linked by curving steps and meandering paths which create a feeling of anticipation: what lovely surprise will be encountered around the next bend? The finishing touch is Bev's skilful plantings, tying the design together. She can be likened to a landscape painter, the garden her vast canvas, forever improving the spectacular scene with a subtle change of colour here, a bit more texture there.

Below right: Orange flowers don't always fit in easily with other colours in the garden, but combine them with ferns and the result, as is shown so well here, is very pleasing indeed. The handsome conifer is *Cedrus atlantica* 'Glauca'.

Opposite: The artificial waterfall tumbles into the big pond with its adjacent summerhouse.

Following pages: Broad steps, their curve pleasing the eye and inviting the feet to climb and explore, provide access through annuals and perennials planted in big drifts to create a natural wildflower look.

A spring morning, with new foliage gleaming, rhododendron flowers sparkling and birds singing their hearts out in the trees: a very special time in one of the great gardens.

Sue and Bill Kay, 'Maru-Wharua', Te Kuiti.

Sue is a very keen gardener, but she has lots of other interests too, so the garden has been designed with ease of maintenance in mind. Huge old deciduous trees, including chestnuts, plane trees, and five huge copper beeches, are a glorious feature throughout the year. Sue loves them most of all in autumn when their leaves turn fiery colours before spiralling earthwards to form a pretty carpet which is later put back on the garden as enriching mulches and compost.

Below: White alyssum, forget-me-nots and angelica provide colour and texture beneath an old horizontal elm.

Rhododendron 'Keay Slocock' is one of the delights of late spring.

Opposite: Close plantings, such as this pretty association of plants beside the house, are favoured because they look natural and reduce the need for weeding.

Vivien and Daniel Papich, 'Bellevue', Langs Beach.

Vivien's love of gardening is so strong she often lies awake at night, plotting new schemes for the garden. In the mornings she and Daniel wake to a view of rose flowers peeking in their bedroom window. Days are taken up with tending or improving their glorious hilltop garden which they have transformed from a "dry, bland bit of clay". Vivien is a strong advocate of the local flora and many of her planting schemes are given added character because natives with dramatic foliage are included among the colourful exotics.

Left: Vivien likes to paint pictures with plants. Among the ingredients of this colourful combination are 'Yellow Wave' flax (on the left), *Verbena peruviana* (brilliant red flowers in middle foreground), Mexican daisy, *Erigeron karvinskianus* (bottom right), hybrid kangaroo paw, *Anigozanthos* (behind and to left of little yellow conifer in centre), renga renga lily, *Arthropodium cirratum* (white flowers at right), and the cream and green foliage of a variegated lacebark, *Hoheria populnea* 'Alba Variegata' (rear).

Masses of cymbidium orchids beside the driveway bear hundreds of flower spikes in the spring.

Photinia 'Red Robin' creates a backdrop for a pretty scene with 'Autumn', one of the four seasons figures, roses, silver leaves of *Stachys byzantina* and white flowers of alyssum.

Right: Glowing pink flowers of the miniature rose 'Pink Cherub' provide prolonged colour at the front of the house. Striking use of foliage plants and amazing coastal views ensure there is year-round interest.

Jill and Bill Maunsell, 'Rahui', Tinui.

Jill's is one of those rambling country gardens where one could linger all day, soaking up the peacefulness of the place, feasting on goodies from a picnic hamper then dozing beneath a magnificent tree. However, any dreams one might have would be hard put to compete with the reality of this garden, where peacocks parade among the old roses and irises, and swans glide by on the pond, their gleaming plumage matched by the flowers of snow white daisies at the water's edge.

Forget-me-nots provide an appropriately casual ground cover beside a woodland path.

Left: A pretty mixed planting of the white daisy *Anthemis cupaniana*, forget-me-nots and arctotis making a frothy mass beneath a kaka beak and leucadendron.

Marguerite Sligh, 'Moat House', Arrowtown.

New Zealand gardens don't get much colder in the winter than Marguerite's, but living close to the mountains means you have spectacular views. The crisp winters kill off a lot of bugs too, so the old roses she loves are wonderfully healthy, and Marguerite is convinced that they have a better perfume than in other, milder regions where she has gardened. 'Moat House' is not just a fanciful name: a stream circles the property.

Opposite: The hardy old rose 'Complicata', a favourite for generations, thrives in the chilly Central Otago winters.

Below: The sunken herb patch, where a surprising range of small edible plants is grown.

A wild rose with the tongue twisting name of *Rosa sericea* subsp. *omeiensis pteracantha* produces a billowing mass of white flowers in early summer. This rose is usually cut back hard every year to encourage lots of the new growth which bears spectacular red thorns, but when allowed to grow into a large bush the flowering display, as can be seen, is nothing short of spectacular.

Toni and Ron Sylvester, 'Omahanui', Greenhithe.

Toni's love of old-fashioned flowers has made 'Omahanui' an enchanted place full of the sights and fragrances of yesteryear. Old roses abound, as do pretty cottage garden perennials, and the garden is enlivened by the gentle calls and fluttering wings of white pigeons. What a contrast to the rows of tired old

The 'Ayrlies Rose' edges the swimming pool.

Left: The brazen garden, where elegant white pigeons compete for attention with the brilliant red flowers of 'Frensham' rose, yellow pokers (kniphofias) and, edging the path, the miniature daylily 'Squeaky'.

Another view of the brazen garden, where yellow daisies scramble among the red 'Frensham' roses and a background pale yellow kangaroo paw *(Anigozanthos flavidus)*.

Opposite: The rose arches, with the big pink flowers of 'Harbinger' and masses of white 'Adelaide d'Orleans'.

Below: Tranquillity awaits at the bottom of the garden, where the predominance of green foliage beneath towering pine trees creates a retreat which is especially popular in the heat of summer.

fruit trees which occupied the land when Toni and Ron bought the property seventeen years ago.

Sally and Bay Allison, 'Lyddington', Rangiora.

It's no surprise to find lots of old roses in Sally's garden, for she has been one of the driving forces behind Heritage Roses New Zealand for some time, but it's astonishing to see how effectively she has used these grand plants. They fill the borders with their scented glory, almost engulf the house, scramble over old tree stumps and ramble over elegant archways, resulting in a garden that's a joy to visit and hard to leave.

Opposite: A great collection of interesting annuals and perennials adds to the considerable character of this garden.

Top left: 'Albéric Barbier', one of Sally's favourite old-fashioned rambling roses, is adored for its lengthy profusion of blooms which have a smell to match their beauty.

Left: Take an old swimming pool and turn it into a large-scale goldfish pond and it becomes a feature of the garden. At the left are the roses 'Francois Juranville' and 'Paul Transon' while to the right is a huge old bush of 'The Fairy'. Outstanding in the centre bed are *Crambe cordifolia* (massed with white flowers), and the roses 'Jean Ducher' (soft pink) and 'Monsieur Tillier' (hot pink).

Gwyn Masters, 'Aramaunga', Stratford.

Gwyn's is one of those charmingly casual Taranaki gardens, where rhododendrons show their love of the rich soils and steady rainfall by growing with casual ease, and wisterias and *Clematis montana* scramble through old trees, creating a cascade of colour in spring. Wisterias trained as standards are a special feature, some of them growing beside the big pond so they can have twice the impact thanks to their reflected glory. It's a garden with personality, created by a petite lady who is much loved for her bubbling enthusiasm and warm manner.

Opposite: A pale wisteria trained as a shrub and the purple-red foliage of a weeping Japanese maple create a scene to linger over beneath a big hawthorn tree.

A 100-year-old wisteria drapes the front of the restored cottage, its fragrance a lovely welcome to late spring visitors. A big clump of libertia sprouts from the paving and a background tree is draped with *Clematis montana* 'Alba', its flowers a similar snow white colour.

Below: Moisture-loving yellow primulas line the pond which was created by damming a stream.

Penny and John Zino, 'Flaxmere', Hawarden.

Gardening's tough at 'Flaxmere', with winters so cold the swimming pool freezes over for days on end, rabbits with an appetite for special plants, ferocious winds and long dry summers. Fortunately Penny and John are people who enjoy a challenge and have responded with a garden which makes the most of the dramatic surroundings and is breathtakingly bold in design.

Top right: Hostas and bergenias provide a lush setting for a little fountain near the house.

Below right: A little garden with an edging of clipped box, providing a lovely contrast to the flowing form of old roses which include 'Fantin Latour' (bright pink, left), 'Trier' (right), 'Devoniensis' (over the archway with white wisteria), and 'Moonlight' (to the left of archway).

Opposite: The garden around the pond is a tranquil spot where moisture-loving plants thrive at the water's edge.

Following pages: The vistas at 'Flaxmere' are art forms.

Felix Jury, 'Tikorangi', Waitara.

Felix doesn't just grow special plants — he creates them too. For more years than he cares to think about he has quietly worked at hybridising hostas, camellias, rhododendrons and magnolias, to name but a few of his specialities. Such are his skills that the resulting plants, among them the wonderful *Magnolia* 'Iolanthe', are acclaimed not just in New Zealand but in many parts of the world. In recent times Felix's son Mark, who also has a special way with plants, has operated a mail order nursery from the gardens so the public can share the joys of the numerous Jury creations.

Top left: Big rhododendrons and tree ferns make for a dramatic spring scene.

Below left: The rare *Hippeastrum aulicum* enjoys shaded conditions, producing its scarlet flowers freely in winter and spring. Also enjoying the conditions are native astelias and the bold variegated foliage *Hosta sieboldiana* 'Aurea Marginata'.

Opposite: In the shade of huge rimus planted by Felix's grandfather last century, striking foliage plants including hostas, native dracophyllums and (in the foreground) the giant Himalayan lily *Cardiocrinum giganteum* combine with colourful azaleas.

Bev and Ken Loader, 'Gethsemane Gardens', Sumner.

Bev and Ken grew vegetables and raised pigs on their hilltop property for thirty-five years before turning it into one of the most talked about gardens in the country. Because the big groups of plants are so spectacular visitors often presume the soil is especially good, but it's actually difficult clay which has been improved over the

Bush daisies provide year-round colour in the sun-drenched garden. This container-grown beauty is 'California Gold', an especially worthwhile dwarf variety.

Right: A design representing the Star of David, created with trimmed hedges of grey and green santolina and buxus.

years by the constant application of all sorts of organic matter, from chicken manure to seaweed. The name of the garden and the religious theme of some of the topiary designs reflect the fact that Ken's a born-again Christian, "and I'm a born-again gardener," says Bev.

Top: Kniphofias are used in big groups, to great effect. 'Dwarf Scarlet' is the foreground variety and 'Bellbird' is at the left.

Below left: An outstanding example of how foliage plants can have as much impact as those grown for their flowers.

Opposite: Big pine trees provide a dramatic backdrop to the garden as well as giving shelter. Gazanias and bush daisies grow beside the steps, with kniphofias in the background.

Jo and Bob Munro, 'Moss Green', Upper Hutt.

'Moss Green' might sound like another of those fanciful names for a garden, but in the case of Bob and Jo it is very descriptive, for they live in a valley where the rainfall in an average year is well over 250 centimetres. Such situations often result in gardens of character and this is certainly the case at 'Moss Green', where little streams and a big pond reflect the surrounding native trees interspersed with the colourful flowers of rhododendrons, Japanese cherries, giant spicy-scented Himalayan lilies *(Cardiocrinum giganteum)*, tall primulas and ground-covering primroses.

Little paths meandering through green and serene native bush, the tranquil sounds of a gentle river nearby, are among the many joys of the Munro garden.

Right: The big snowy blossoms of 'Shirotae' (formerly 'Mt Fuji'), one of the most spectacular of the beautiful Japanese cherries, and rhododendrons 'Blue Diamond' and 'Ivanhoe' near the pond.

Liz and Richard Luisetti, Rangiora.

Liz is a gentle Englishwoman with strong ideas on what makes a garden beautiful. Her town garden is a place of wonder, particularly in early summer when roses and perennials are at their glorious peak. Richard looks after the

Below: The rose 'Penelope', a wonderful hybrid musk raised by retired English clergyman Joseph Pemberton in the early 1900s, delights with its scent, beauty, attractive habit of growth and long flowering period. In Liz and Richard's garden it combines charmingly with a small-flowered cistus.

Right: The red bed, Liz's protest at the fashion for pale colours. 'Chianti' is in the centre foreground, the scarlet blooms of 'Altissimo' can be glimpsed at the right, bronze fennel provides a dusky foliage contrast and cream-flowered 'Mme Alfred Carrière' is swagged on chains held up by posts which are a reminder that once this glorious area of the garden was a tennis court.

vegetable area which is as beautiful as it is productive, proving that edible crops can fit easily into an artistic garden.

Left: A brick path leads the eye to this charming lady at the back of the house. Either side of the path are free-flowering plants such as pansies, hardy geraniums, heucheras and Mexican daisies. The roses in varying shades of golden-yellow are 'Whisky', 'Western Sun' and 'Peace'.

Below: The big blooms of the old rose 'Golden Wings' are made even more interesting by the background haze of catmint. The fuchsia-like shrub *Phygelius aequalis*, which flowers all summer, is to the right of 'Golden Wings' and the scarlet rose on the left is 'Altissimo'.

Sue and John Dalziell, 'Grassendale', Tinui.

Sue and John started with two established silver birches and lots of grass surrounding a rundown house. From these unpromising beginnings they have created one of the Wairarapa's most noted gardens, full of old roses, perennials and handsome trees; a place with that "far from the worries of the world" atmosphere that is a characteristic of the best country gardens. Sue isn't resting on her laurels now that the garden is established — she's got her eye on the surrounding hills and is contemplating how nice it would be to have them clothed with ornamental trees.

Top left: The pretty new leaves of a maple *Acer* 'Brilliantissimum', the white daisy *Anthemis cupaniana* edging the path and masses of red candelabra primulas in the low-lying boggy area make for springtime enchantment.

Below left: Pale coloured stone from a local river has been used most effectively for walls and steps. *Anthemis cupaniana* hangs over the wall and *Robinia* 'Frisia', one of the most popular foliage trees, provides a golden contrast.

Opposite: Forget-me-nots, appreciated for their natural look, run riot in a woodland area beneath silver birches, rhododendrons and hydrangeas.

Elizabeth and Graham Robertson, 'Crosshills', Otorohanga.

Let a florist with flair loose on a bare piece of land and the result will be a garden of stunning design such as we have at 'Crosshills'. Former florist Elizabeth, helped by husband and sons, was in her element creating this garden. Now it gives joy to visitors from far and wide and is even seen on television screens in the Northern Hemisphere — not so long ago a film crew from London turned up and shot a commercial in the garden!

Top right: The architectural form of giant hogweed complements the yellow spires of verbascum and a rugged stone wall where 'Fluffy' the family cat likes to promenade. (Giant hogweed is a plant to handle with care — some people are extremely allergic to its sap.)

Right centre: The house is as big a talking point as the garden. Built to look as if it has stood for generations, it is comparatively new. Free-flowering Mexican daisy softens the bold, weathered sleeper steps in the foreground.

Below right: A pair of *Robinia* 'Frisia' losing their autumn cloak of gold.

Opposite: A reminder that one of the often overlooked advantages of a lawn is the wonderful shadows cast on it by trees.

The astonishing foliage of green and cream kale and a yellow topiary conifer trained to resemble a wedding cake are features of a border which says it all about Elizabeth's skill and daring when it comes to the use of plants. The golden foliage of *Robinia* 'Frisia' to the rear is echoed by perennials including *Helichrysum bracteatum* and *Helianthus* 'Golden Pyramid' in the border.

Left: Flowing lines of walls and paving and skilfully balanced plantings are a highlight of this very artistic garden.

Below: A formal area, with lavender bordering beds of roses.

Daphne and Hugh Wilson, 'Matai Moana', Gore Bay.

Daphne and Hugh have transformed what was once a weed infested sand-hill into one of the most glorious seaside gardens in New Zealand. They didn't stop at turning their own garden into a beauty spot, taking the adjacent public walkway under their wing as well so that brilliant flowers now extend almost to the high tide mark. As if that weren't enough, Hugh is a dedicated vegetable gardener who produces enormous crops from his allotment up the road.

Opposite: It is hard to believe that this was an erosion-prone sand bank a few years ago. Now it's a mass of groundcover plants which stabilise as well as beautify. In the foreground are orange wallflowers, blue *Convolvulus mauritanicus*, pink pelargoniums, pink and white iberis, and nasturtiums.

Below: Proof that beautiful gardens can be created close to the sea.

Beach gardens are all about bright colour and on this bank the cheerful scene is provided by pelargoniums and succulents, with the cream and orange trumpets of *Brugmansia sanguinea* (datura) at the rear.

Barbara and Ric Toogood, 'Reviresco', Havelock North.

Barbara, widely admired for her skilful combinations of plants, likes a garden to be restful, something she achieves through a blending of colours. She also aims for year-round interest in her garden. Her wonderful results have been achieved in spite of "shocking" soil which is constantly being coaxed to perform beyond expectations with lots of organic mulches and fertiliser.

The view from the house is of restful green foliage and white flowers complementing the elegant pond.

Left: A border beside the drive with pink heuchera flowers tumbling over white alyssum at the front, backed up by yellow achilleas, delphiniums and nicotianas.

99

On a fence beside the front gate the
little pink-flowered rose 'Ballerina' is
almost constantly in flower. Next to it is
a rose which Barbara purchased as the
'Gerbe Rose'.

Right: A tree in decline and a youthful
rose full of vigour create a dramatic
picture. The rose is 'Bantry Bay'.

Below: 'Champneys Pink Cluster' rose
grows on the posts above a carpet of
violas, and 'Wedding Day' climbs
through a background poplar. The lime
green and pink flowers glimpsed in the
distance are nicotianas and heucheras.

Murray Chick and Alastair Pearson, 'Earthsea Gardens', Matapouri Bay.

'Surf Rider', one of many hibiscus in the garden, produces its flamboyant flowers for months on end.

'**E**arthsea' is like a scene from a romantic novel set in the South Seas. A garden full of brightly coloured flowers, mouth-watering fruits, giant bamboos, perfectly shaped palm trees, a hammock strung in a shady corner, the climate blissfully mild all year; if only our responsibilities were fewer we would leave in search of such a place tomorrow!

Below: Bold foliage plants such as the cabbage tree and a pony tail palm *(Beaucarnea recurvata)* in front of the house and the background mountain paw paw provide year-round interest.

Opposite: Waterlily-filled ponds and background palm trees help to create the image of a tropical jungle paradise.

Susanna and Christopher Grace, 'Rathmoy', Hunterville.

Susanna is one of those optimistic gardeners, always planning for next season. There are no disasters in her garden — if something dies it is regarded as a golden opportunity to plant something interesting in its place. 'Rathmoy' is a garden with a sense of fun, as anyone who has seen the delightful scarecrow which presides over the vegetable garden will agree. All sorts of animals, both in the garden and the adjoining paddocks, add to the feeling of informality. As Susanna says, you can't take yourself too seriously when you have animals in a garden.

Opposite: The big purple flower heads of *Geranium maderense*, blue catmint, old roses, white valerian, mignonette and hardy geraniums flow together like a scene from a dreamy watercolour painting.

Top left: Rose 'Uetersen' shows its considerable charms on an archway leading to the vegetable garden. This is a rose which earns Susanna's highest praise — it flowers incredibly freely, needs little attention, and the wonderful shade of pink inspires her to create all sorts of colour schemes.

Left: Looking towards the entry gate from the house with a big clump of blue *Hosta sieboldiana* prominent, behind it a pink bush daisy, then snow in summer (cerastium) in a container, an interesting change from its usual habit of spreading rather too rapidly as a ground cover.

Muriel and Bob Davison, 'Maple Glen', Wyndham.

'Maple Glen' is one of those amazing rural gardens which seems to have extended a little further into the surrounding paddocks every time you visit. Unlike some farm gardens, it is no haphazard extension, for Muriel is both plantswoman and artist, with a keen eye for what makes a dramatic scene and

Hosta sieboldiana seedlings, their lush growth an indication of their liking for the Southland soils and climate, form a striking edging for a grass path.

Right: The conifer and heather garden, where there is year-round interest. The rare yellow form of *Pinus radiata* towers in the background. The golden blooms of *Euryops acraeus* brighten the foreground across the path from the slender form of *Juniperus* 'Blue Heaven'.

which plants look most effective together. As the name suggests, 'Maple Glen' contains a lot of maples. It is also home to an incredible collection of birds, many of them flying free, for Muriel knows as much about them as she does her plants, and perhaps loves them even more.

Opposite: A perfect example of how effective plants with bold foliage (gunneras, *Astelia chathamica*, variegated pampas — *Cortaderia selloana* 'Gold Band') look beside water. Numerous ponds have been created in the garden and are now home for a wide range of water birds, from glamorous white swans to humble ducks.

Top left: A daring colour combination of the purple hardy *Geranium ibericum*, an orange candelabra primula and bright yellow *Calceolaria integrifolia*.

Left centre: 'Nellie Moser', a superb hybrid clematis, provides the ultimate disguise for an old tree stump.

Below left: Looking towards the house, with clumps of *Iris sibirica* in the foreground, *Prunus nigra* making a mass of purple-red and the vast rock garden beneath the recently remodelled house.

Ann Bond, Waitara.

There is a feeling of peace, a restfulness, about Ann's garden, achieved by the use of foliage plants as a backdrop to soft coloured flowers. It's very much a family garden too, where weddings and other happy events are celebrated.

Top right: Pink foxgloves, blue granny bonnets and *Diascia rigescens*, chosen because their pretty flowers co-ordinate with the colour scheme of the house.

Below right: There is a deliberate contrast between the garden and the surrounding paddocks which can be glimpsed through the fence.

Opposite: Elegant hostas provide superb ground cover beside a path leading to a moon gate made from recycled timber.

Geoff Haughey and Richard Cadness, 'Westridge', Titirangi.

Geoff and Richard weren't sure how to develop a garden beneath the towering nikaus and giant kauris when they first bought their paradise in the Waitakere Ranges. Then they saw the Rhododendron Dell at Kew Gardens

Camellia 'Donation', with the white flowers of *Camellia* 'Coronation' in the background.

Right: The glorious steps are as functional as they are beautiful, providing easy access during the winter. Wood pigeons flock to the garden when the berries of the big nikau palms ripen.

while on holiday in England and realised that these flamboyant shrubs were the ideal understorey planting for the giants back home. So they began the task of developing their unique and truly outstanding garden, overcoming the problems of sticky clay along the way. It took a while, but to quote a favourite saying of Richard's from the Koran, "With patience, success."

Top right: Beside paths and underneath the tall nikau palms, clivias enliven many a shady area, their glowing flowers set off to perfection by the fronds of native ferns such as the hen and chickens fern, *Asplenium bulbiferum*.

Right centre: Late summer colour courtesy of Japanese anemones and impatiens.

Below right: *Rhododendron* 'Britannia' glows in the shadows.

Opposite: Rhododendrons thrive as an understorey to towering tree ferns and nikau palms. At the back is 'Mrs J.P. Lade', in the centre 'Mrs A.T. de la Mare' and in front *Azalea splendens*.

Alan and Catherine Trott, 'Trotts Garden and Nursery', Ashburton.

A great collection of foliage plants means that the garden of Alan and Catherine is interesting throughout the year. Water gardens surrounded by lush moisture-loving perennials are one of the garden's highlights — another is grand herbaceous borders on a scale reminiscent of famous English gardens. Even winter brings its joys, such as the quiet beauty of deciduous trees grown for their outstanding bark.

Below: The belvedere provides views of garden delights, including the creek and bog area which is home to moisture lovers such as bold blue-grey-leaved *Hosta sieboldiana* and *Ligularia stenocephala* 'The Rocket', which is in the process of putting up its distinctive black-stemmed flower spikes.

Gently curving grass paths create a desire to see what surprises lie around the corner. Bold foliage perennials such as bronze ligularia and hostas contrast with shrubs of diverse form, including a deutzia and the weeping red Japanese maple on the corner.

Opposite: The ghostly white trunk of a very special birch tree *(Betula jacquemontii)* is an upper crust companion for hostas, dicentras and a yellow berberis near the pond.

Shirley and Ian Greenhill, Stratford.

The sound of running water is always an attraction in a garden and at Shirley and Ian's a sparkling stream surging over a little waterfall draws people like a magnet. The edges of the stream are planted with moisture-loving plants while further back, where the drainage is better, azaleas and rhododendrons, often planted so they create big drifts of colour, make a memorable picture. It is hard to believe that a little over two decades ago this paradise was a tangle of convolvulus running riot over old willow stumps. It just goes to show that keen gardeners will overcome virtually any obstacles.

Top left: The winding paths are edged with flowerng plants that provide a spectacle in spring. In this area yellow candelabra primulas and foxgloves make an enchanting foreground to the big red *Rhododendron* 'Red Glow.'

Below left: The grey foliage of *Hosta sieboldiana* makes a superb combination with pink primulas and the new foliage of a large-leaved rhododendron.

Opposite: The stream is one of this garden's special features, its banks planted with moisture-loving plants such as hostas and candelabra primulas.

Nan and Wynne Raymond, Timaru.

"It was a blank canvas except for the old oak trees and some huge roses," says Nan of her garden when she started work on it ten years ago. With a vision of what the garden would become, she had extremely high brick walls built to divide it and create stunning vistas. Then the big herbaceous borders were planted in a style which shows she is a gifted garden artist with exceptional colour sense.

Opposite: The sweetly scented hybrid musk roses 'Penelope' and 'Felicia' take centre stage in a dramatic border of flowers, with foxgloves and delphiniums towering alongside the roses and silver-leaved stachys in flower on the edge beside *Alchemilla mollis*.

The rose arbour, designed by Nan, with penstemons, foxgloves and the silver foliage of *Stachys byzantina*.

Below: Looking across the pond, with blue campanulas in the foreground, and lots of roses including 'Purity' on the archway in the middle, 'Iceberg' either side and pretty pink 'Clair Matin'.

Exuberant 'Wedding Day', a modern rambler rose with old-fashioned charm, at its elegant best.

Left: A gorgeous silver pear *(Pyrus salicifolia* 'Pendula') terminates the view between mirror image plantings of stachys, alchemilla, roses, delphiniums and nigella.

Below: The inspired combination of bold, gold 'Graham Thomas' roses, blue delphiniums, *Alchemilla mollis*, and nigella in front of one of the tall brick walls which divide the garden.

Bronwyn and Doug Thornycroft, Nelson.

Bronwyn and Doug developed their garden to suit their old-fashioned house and to blend with the surroundings of farm and mountains. The high altitude results in crisp winters and tricky late frosts but by growing plants which are hardy, and carefully positioning those which might be marginally so, they have a lovely show in spring and summer. On the edge of the garden towering beeches, among the most majestic of native forest trees, create a wonderland where one can wander in nature's garden and escape the cares of the world.

Top right: The high altitude is very much to the liking of native alpine plants such as these exquisite mountain daisies *(Celmisia coriacea)*.

Right centre: Walkways have been created through the several hectares of beech forest which make a beautiful backdrop to the garden.

Below right: Hostas proved a great success beneath a huge old walnut tree, standing the dry conditions surprisingly well and loving the shade.

Opposite: The edge of the beech trees has proved to be an ideal spot for rhododendrons, which would lose their buds to the late frosts if grown in the open. *Rhododendron* 'Pink Pearl' is in the foreground.

Peter and Norma Murphy, 'Panikau', Gisborne.

Visiting 'Panikau', tucked away in the hills north of Gisborne, is like stepping back in time to an age when amazing gardens on remote farms were the norm. Work on the garden in its present form began in 1918 when Alfred Buxton, in his time New Zealand's foremost landscape architect, was

The elegant but hardy *Styrax japonica*, which provides considerable pleasure with its handsome form, pretty white flowers in spring and, as is shown so clearly here, colourful autumn foliage.

Left: The pink flowers of schizostylis add to the joys of autumn. Some of the extensive stone walls and rock gardens can be glimpsed in the background.

engaged by Peter's grandfather to create and oversee the design. Stonemasons spent two years building a series of stone walls (280 metres of them), pergolas and rock gardens which are such a feature of this lovingly restored garden.

Opposite: Fiery tints of Boston ivy *(Parthenocissus tricuspidata* 'Veitchii').

Above right: The historic, wisteria-draped pergola made from stone quarried on the property.

Below: The modern home, designed to blend in with the surroundings, stands on the site of the original homestead which burnt down in 1981. A weeping Japanese maple wearing its autumn cloak and the violet flowers of *Limonium perezii* provide foreground interest.

Sally Marshall and Peter Spencer, 'The Ridges', Marton.

'The Ridges' is reminiscent of a grand English garden, and in the tradition of such gardens it has remained in the same family for a very long time. Sally Marshall is the enthusiastic third-generation custodian of this special place and the borders are full of the perennials she adores. When they flower in spring, beneath the magnificent rhododendrons and azaleas her grandmother planted, the garden is especially fascinating, while the grand old trees are a year-round feature.

Below: Huge deciduous azaleas fill the garden with fiery colour in November.

Centrepiece of the sunken garden is 'Spring' (one of the four seasons figures) which Sally's grandparents brought back from England in the 1950s.

Opposite: A handsome herring-bone pattern brick path leads to the delights of the sunken garden.

Liz and Geoff Brunsden, 'Windrest Cottage', Te Puke.

L iz and Geoff took a derelict orchard, turned it into a rambling romantic garden with a feel of yesteryear and opened it to the public. The just over half a hectare offers great variety, from glorious roses and spectacular wild-flowers to tranquil woodlands. The popularity of the garden can be gauged from the number of visitors who return time and again. Some even get married

The glow of red mollis azaleas among lush foliage.

Right: Masses of colour co-ordinated perennials and roses border the croquet lawn.

on the big lawn, where croquet is played and there is maypole dancing in spring. And how did they come up with the lovely name of 'Windrest'? It's derived from the name of their street, 'Moehau', which translates loosely as the place of the sleeping wind.

Opposite: The tall stems of pretty *Silene dioica* line one of the numerous intimate paths.

A brilliant corner with orange and red deciduous azaleas in front of a grand specimen of 'The Bishop', an old gallica rose with nicely scented flowers.

Top left: The flowers of a hybrid rhododendron *(R. lindleyi* x *nuttallii* x *dalhousiae)* bear an enticing spicy fragrance.

Below left: The pretty deciduous shrub *Weigela florida* 'Variegata' at its spring peak.

Peter and Elizabeth Ormond, 'Ormonds Garden and Nursery', Havelock North.

If plants aren't able to cope with the summer heat, low rainfall conditions and the strictly observed no watering rule in this garden then they don't get a look in. The result is a wonderful example for people in dry areas of what trees, shrubs and perennials (they don't grow any cacti) will be successful in their gardens without the need for pampering. And many of the plants seen in the display gardens are available from the small on-site nursery.

Below: Foliage plants, including the excellent and adaptable *Heuchera* 'Palace Purple', beneath the trees.

Purple culinary sage, yellow totara and the white flowers and silver foliage of *Tanacetum* 'Silver Lace' enliven a mixture of drought-tolerant plants.

Opposite: Plants have to be tough to grow here without any supplementary water once they are put in the ground, but it's surprising how many relish the conditions.

Joyce and John Clyne, 'Tally Ho', Matamata.

It's obvious from the moment that one enters Joyce's garden that here is someone who loves plants and has an ability to arrange them with imagination. Joyce's eye for colour shows up in her groupings of plants and her use of rhodohypoxis in big drifts illustrates how effective a lot of one type of plant can be. One of her great concerns is to achieve a good cover of plants: "I don't like to see bare earth in a garden."

The lovely full look of the colour co-ordinated cottage border. A pair of Chinese toon trees *(Cedrela sinensis)* show off their bright pink spring foliage at the end of the garden.

Opposite: The big bed of rhodohypoxis started out as a handful of bulbs brought from Joyce's old garden — in ten years she has steadily increased them to the stage where they make the present spectacular show. The flowers continue for three months, starting in late September.

Below: *Viburnum* 'Roseace' makes a stunning contrast in the middle of a group of deciduous azaleas.

Pauline and John Trengrove, Sir Miles Warren, 'Ohinetahi', Governors Bay.

Starting from a wilderness, working with a clear vision of what the garden would become, this talented trio of two architects and a painter have created a garden which is widely regarded as one of the best in the world. As is the way with very special

A superb piece of bold garden design, creating a feeling of drama. Like a wonderful painting, the eye is immediately drawn to a point of great interest (up the steps to the container framed by a gap in the pleached hornbeam work), then leisurely takes in all the interesting surroundings.

Right: The striking long vistas are a special feature of 'Ohinetahi'. This one extends from the formal rose garden, the paths edged with little buxus hedges, down the length of a rectangular pond and through a pair of Irish yews to a distant focal point.

achievements, it took a lot of hard work along the way — Pauline recalls laying bricks most weekends for several years and thinking the task would never come to an end. But all the important foundation work did conclude in time, and the carefully chosen plants grew despite the poor soil, culminating in a supreme example of garden design as an art form.

A corner of the white garden, with clipped box (buxus) hedging tying the design together. The house, seen in the background, was one of the first large dwellings to be built in the area and well over a century later is still in beautiful condition.

Left: Rugged hills provide a fittingly dramatic backdrop to an astonishing garden.

Margaret and Hamish McKegg, Hamilton.

Margaret and Hamish's garden is a lovely peaceful place, bordering the slow moving waters of the Waikato River. The colours of the garden have been carefully chosen with the river views in mind: lots of foliage and not too many bright flowers so that the plantings complement rather than compete with the backdrop of water. Gardening is tough going here — the land is pure pumice and before any plant goes into the ground a big hole has to be dug out and filled with lots of topsoil and compost.

Top right: An unnamed apricot rose tumbles among *Euphorbia veneta* (formerly *E. wulfeni)* with *Echium* "Blue Bedder" at the left.

Below right: The bright red new foliage of *Pieris* 'Lord Wakehurst' ties in with the flowers of a background rhododendron. A dense edging of hostas completes the picture. Margaret uses hostas extensively, finding their beautifully textured foliage and pale summer flowers very restful.

Opposite: The subtle colours of white foxgloves, pale gold wallflowers, white lychnis and pale yellow lysimachia provide a pretty complement to the river which is the climax of the garden.

Gordon and Annette Collier, 'Titoki Point', Taihape.

Gordon is a connoisseur of hardy plants. 'Titoki Point', his hillside garden in the central high country, contains an amazing collection of the special and rare, many of them imported during the last thirty years from the best nurseries in the world. Gordon differs from many a plant fanatic in his artistic eye which ensures the plants are shown off to good advantage. This has been appreciated by gardeners around the world — in addition to the thousands of folk who have visited Gordon and

Opposite: A garden of special plants arranged in a very pleasing way. *Hosta* 'Gold Tiara', *Rhododendron* 'Ostbo's Red Elizabeth', *Ajuga reptans* 'Alba' and *Enkianthus perulatus* provide the foreground interest.

Rhododendron 'Charlotte de Rothschild' among hostas, hellebores and ferns at the bottom of the garden.

Annette at 'Titoki Point', the garden has been filmed by numerous overseas television crews and shown in North America, England and Australia.

Below: Looking towards the silver birch grove, with the white flowers of *Deutzia* 'Nikko' in the centre. The plant with green maple-like leaves in the left foreground is *Glaucidium palmatum*.

Helen and Don Russell, 'Brackenbank', Amberley.

Beautiful 'Brackenbank' looks as if it has stepped from the pages of a book on romantic English gardens. This isn't entirely a coincidence, for Helen and Don have been inspired by the creations of some of Britain's most innovative gardeners, but they have added their own ideas and the result is a truly inspired "retirement" garden.

Right: A few years ago this area was an eyesore — a muddy hollow where there had once been a big cattle trough. It was dug out and made into this big pond, creating a wonderful reflecting surface and a home for waterlilies and goldfish galore.

The borders are wonderful examples of how well thought out combinations of plants are truly works of art. Looking along the border we see hot pink *Cistus* 'Brilliancy', white valerian, red valerian (*Centranthrus ruber* and *C. r.* 'Alba'), Russell lupins and the old rose 'Tausendschön' (which gains in appeal even more when one realises the translation is 'Thousand Beauties') on the background fence.

Following pages: The wonderful rose archway is designed to frame the view beyond as well as provide a means of showing off old-fashioned climbing roses to perfection. It's a place to linger, the senses heightened by the gorgeous fragrance and stimulating beauty of 'Albéric Barbier' (left), 'Leschenaultii' (right), and pink 'Clair Matin' (the smaller plant at right in front of 'Leschenaultii').

148

Anne and Maurice McGregor, 'Tui Grange', Matamata.

Anne believes that if a garden is to be successful it must tie in with the house, a philosophy which has guided her development of the remarkable 'Tui Grange'. To visit this garden is to enter another world, a place with incredible views, wonderful birdlife and special plants chosen for their texture and foliage as much as their flowers.

Top right: The remarkably free-flowering shrubby perennial *Lavatera* 'Barnsley' is its usual mass of pink in late summer, adding to the joys of salvias, asters, gaueras and impatiens.

Right centre: A sun-drenched bank is the perfect spot for a cheery assortment of perennial daisies.

Below right: Autumn tints of a Japanese maple contrast with cool greens in a shady corner.

Opposite: When your garden is 800 metres above sea level one of the advantages is dramatic views.

Gay and John Rutherford, 'Gola Peaks', Hawarden.

A way in the South Island high country, surrounded by tussock grass and mountains, battling heavy winter snowfalls and short growing seasons, Gay has created a garden which is astonishing. It's a garden made with a sensitive feel for the beautiful yet harsh environment and its special colourings. It's also a garden created with a limited palette of plants, for not everything likes to grow in such a climate.

Opposite: The rough hewn look of wooden steps provides a striking contrast in texture to the surrounding plants. The gorgeous purple-blue and grey effect is created by the flowers of *Lavandula stoechas*, bearded irises and centaurea and the foliage of *Stachys byzantina* (foreground) and *Senecio greyii* (at the rear).

A serene path through the woodland area with a horse chestnut and *Senecio greyii*.

Below: A sunny path behind the house with the wonderfully adaptable daisy *Anthemis cupaniana* in the foreground.

John and Fiona Wills, 'Trelinnoe Park', Te Pohue.

This vast garden started out as a modest planting around a farm house and expanded to become 10 hectares (25 acres) of glorious flowering and foliage trees, broad landscaped lawns and intimate woodland paths, clipped hedges and extensive vistas. The moods change with the seasons and visitors often debate which is the most enchanting time. Some rate the early spring, when the huge collection of magnolias put on a breathtaking display, as the best time to visit, while others regard autumn as the most magical. Whatever the season, it's a shining example of New Zealand gardening at its best.

Rhododendron 'Janet Blair' is a cascade of pink in spring.

Opposite: Vistas of rolling farmland add to the large-scale feel of the garden.

Below: Clipped hedges are a trademark of 'Trelinnoe'.

A soldier-like row of *Picea albertiana*.

Below right: *Salvia mexicana* beneath pin oak trees which have been limbed up to make the most of the expansive views. The tall umbrella of foliage provides a bit of relief from the baking Hawke's Bay summer sun.

Preceding pages: Large numbers of deciduous trees turn stunning colours in the autumn.